How to Live an Empowered Life

Easy and Practical Daily Tools

Lisa A. Barrett, LPC, ATR

ISBN: 979-8-218-55374-6

LCCN: 2024924136

Lisa A. Barrett, LPC, ATR
Cover Image and Design
Interior Images

Book Design and Editing
Bannon River Books, LLC – Colleen Brunetti

Printed in the United States of America

10 9 8 7 6 5 4 3 2 1

Endorsements

Would you like a therapist in your pocket? This is it! Full of sage, yet tactile and practical, advice to steer your life toward abundance and joy.

~ *Dr. Bridget Cooper, Cage Rattler & Author of Unflappable.*

How to Live an Empowered Life is ideal for anyone seeking a straightforward, non-intimidating introduction to the principles of self-empowerment. Its clear language and focus on simple repeatable actions make it a valuable resource for those feeling overwhelmed by life's circumstances, and who are looking to gain a sense of inner control and what the author calls *Calm Clarity*. I suggest you pick up your copy today, and start feeling better right away.

~ *Dan Blanchard, Bestselling Author of The Storm, TEDX, Professional Teen Leadership Speaker, President: National Speakers Association-CT, President: Association of Publishers for Special Sales, Host of Mindalia TV*

Easy read, packed with unlimited power to transform and live a better live.

~*Thierry Huck, MSW, ACSW, LCSW*

You can't help but take slower, deeper breaths as you read this book. Here you'll find the tools and strategies you need to establish a practice of connecting to the skills that lie within you, and that will empower you to cope with the external forces we all face.

~*Debra Cassidy, M. Ed.*

Lisa reminds us that self-awareness isn't selfish—it's how we contribute to the collective good. As a coach who has studied human and organizational behavior and worked with individuals, Fortune 500 companies, universities, and non-profits for more than 20 years, I deeply appreciate her invitation to intentional self-reflection. Lisa's work inspires us to tune our inner frequency toward clarity, compassion, and empowerment—pathways not only to personal fulfillment but to our shared communal well-being.

~*Stacey Zackin, PhD, MSW, PCC, founder of theCoach4you, a values-based Life and Leadership Coaching practice*

Contents

Also By Lisa A. Barrett

Laughter, Wisdom, and Innocence:
Surprising Quotes From Children

Available on Amazon.

This book ranked #1 New Release in School-Age Children and Parenting and ranked #1 out of 100 in Kindle store in the following 4 categories:
#1 in Child Psychology
#1 in Adolescent Psychology
#1 in Emotions & Mental Health
#1 in Parenting, Emotions & Feelings

Foreword

In the late 90's I read the book *Real Magic: How to Create Miracles in Everyday Life* by author and counselor, Wayne W. Dyer. It changed my life completely. Now I've found the sequel to that book, the one you're holding in your hands by Licensed Professional Counselor, Lisa A. Barrett. *How to Live an Empowered Life* lays out the action plan one needs to go on creating everyday miracles that won't just help build a beautiful life, but will help you influence those in your circle to create their own miracles.

Lisa shows us that it is easy to feel controlled by external forces such as people, places, things and especially situations. The tools you learn will prevent you from becoming the *walking dead,* people driven by fear of external forces. *How to Live an Empowered Life* will lay out a simple to follow plan for thinking and behaving in ways that move you closer to the power of love instead.

Being afraid of failure is one of those external powers that is inflated by the energy associated with fear. One becomes paralyzed and unable to live a productive life. You will learn how you may allow yourself to be held hostage to the feelings of fear of failure. The details provided will help the reader see the secrets to unbuckling themselves from this destructive force by offering solutions to choosing a more productive relationship with perceived failure.

I always share with parents in my classes that feelings aren't right or wrong, they just are. In this book, Lisa provides the answers to changing the readers perspective on feelings and how just allowing them to exist from a neutral point of view can create miracles for themselves and others.

Finally, I highly recommend reading this book because you will walk away with some powerful gifts that will change your life. My favorite one is how Lisa defines reacting simply to information. When someone walks up to you and hits you hard with criticism, we are likely to react negatively by getting defensive and even wanting to fight back and get even. But as Lisa teaches you, the power begins by coming from a neutral position and seeing the criticism as simply information. The next time you find yourself on the receiving end, try her suggestion and say to your critic, *"Isn't that interesting..."* and not attach yourself to emotions.

~ Bill Corbett

Radio talk show host and author of the book, "Love, Limits & Lessons: A Parent's Guide to Raising Cooperative Kids"

http://CooperativeKids.com

The Empowered Self

It's not just about redefining your life
Its about being 100% committed to it
With your intentions, thoughts, feelings, faith,
And trust

Embrace what you don't know
Step into the great mystery
Where unlimited potentiality lives
Within you

Let fear of the unknown be a fleeting thought
Refuse to compromise on your dreams, desires
And happiness

What you focus on will grow
So choose to plant seeds of joy
Take action steps forward regularly
And the rest will unfold
In ways you never thought possible

~Lisa

From the Author

I'd like to thank the universal forces that aligned with my own personal creation, for my life's journey of wondrous adventures and joy, as well as life altering years of trauma. Everything that I teach and share with others I truly live daily to the fullest. For had I not walked through my own darkness, I would not have been able to touch and heal so many along the way. Without those experiences, this book would not have been possible and I would not have discovered what it is to truly live an empowered life.

~Lisa

Chapter One

Introduction

I strongly believe learning empowerment is key to a more fulfilled and well adjusted life. Learning empowerment can feel like a big undertaking, but it doesn't have to be. I wrote this book with the intention of providing a quick guide of inspirational, factual, clinical, and practical information and skills, which can easily be used in your daily life.

Although self-help books are wonderful, they are often lengthy. The key word here is lengthy. One must use a notebook to write down everything that resonates with them so they won't forget what they read. It often takes a while to get through the book and by then applying the new information can be difficult.

I am a Licensed Professional Counselor and a Registered Art Therapist, and I purposefully wanted to condense much of what I teach with my clients, and utilize in my own daily life to a quick practical short read. I draw upon my many years of personal experiences, academic background, clinical practice, spiritual wisdom, and mindful based disciplines. Because life is a daily practice of self-care, and self-love, I hope this book serves as a quick and easy reminder when you go a little off course.

"When writing the story of your life, never let anyone hold the pen."
~Harley Davidson

"Everything in your life can be done better when you come from Calm Clarity (C.C.)."
~ Lisa A. Barrett

Chapter Two

Emotional Frequencies

What exactly are *emotional frequencies*? If you're not familiar, the phrase may sound like they are something unreal. I assure you, they are not! Our whole universe is made up of energy, and we humans are no different! I reference lower vibrational frequencies (LVF) and higher vibrational frequencies (HVF) often in this book. We ourselves are vibrational beings. The very law of vibration[1] is a fundamental principle in the universe, which states that animate and inanimate objects vibrate with energy. Science teaches us that nothing is solid, even when it appears to be when seen with the human eye.

The fact that everything is in constant motion helps us to understand the role emotional frequencies have in our lives. Individual frequencies are emitted through our thoughts, beliefs, emotions and actions. Vibrations from your energetic frequencies determine what is attracted back to you. All emotions are fleeting. Some stay longer than others, and as you will learn, this can be a choice.

Higher Vibrational Frequencies (HVF) vs. Lower Vibrational Frequencies (LVF)

Love based emotions may include: love, joy, gratitude, passion, kindness, creativity, calmness, etc. and are associated with higher vibrational frequencies (HVF). When you feel these, it is an indicator you are living from your heart, your truth and your source.

Fear based emotions may include: anger, fear, guilt, shame, sadness, anxiety, jealousy, etc. and are associated with lower vibrational frequencies (LVF). Although we may all feel them from time to time which is a normal human experience, know that emotions are temporary no matter how intense they may feel. Our job is to accept them and shift them. [2]

Chapter Three

Disempowerment

Before we can learn the skills and tools that allow us to become empowered in all areas of our life, we need to define disempowerment. Disempowerment stems from allowing people, places, things or situations to control you. Going forward, these will be referred to as *externals*.

Will people, places, things or situations affect us? Yes! But the extent of how we view the externals, and to what level of emotions and thoughts we attach to them, is what will drive our outcome either way. This is where disempowerment takes hold. Thoughts become real. Attachment to the externals will get you in trouble.

"The root of all suffering is attachment."
~The Buddha

We sink our claws in and hold on tightly to externals: what that person will think of us, if your car doesn't start how it will ruin your day, the government is to blame, the weather is bad, another person is to blame.

Blaming others is the biggest delusion of all. It matters not who is the primary person at fault because on a deeper level (subconsciously for most) you are part of creating all of what you are experiencing.

The number one way to disempower yourself, no matter what the situation, is by putting all your energy on blaming. You in essence are saying, *All the externals control me, I have no control of my thoughts, actions, reactions, situation, finances, relationships, health, career, and the list goes on.*

Being in a state of *reaction* comes from emotionality. Emotionality comes from being triggered by something that is unsettled in us. Sentences that include the words, *he made me, she made me*, and *they made me* couldn't be more disempowering.

Choosing to react instead of taking responsibility for your life is the largest injustice you can ever do to yourself.

Chapter Four

Poor Me

When you fall into a rut of *poor me* thinking, you are riding a downward spiral of true disempowerment. Here are just some examples of *poor me* thinking:

"Why do things always happen to me?" or *"No one will help me, hire me, love me, etc."* When you think about these feelings, how do they feel? Usually not good.

Let's be more specific about the feelings these thoughts can invoke: depression, helplessness, disempowerment, anger, overwhelm, frustration, and decreased motivation, just to name a few. Perhaps you have some words of your own you would add to this list.

The above emotions have lower vibrational frequencies (LVF). We are made of energy which responds to our emotional state, thus causing a physiological response in our body. As such, victim mentality can cause several chain reactions in your sympathetic nervous system.

Your immune system becomes slower and less efficient so it decreases its ability to ward off sickness; which in turn increases and then validates the *poor me* emotions. When one is preoccupied with the LVF you can find yourself taking on all sorts of unhealthy behaviors: overeating, overspending, disconnecting in relationships, sleeping more, staring at the screens more, not doing the activities you used to enjoy, sub-stance use and abuse, lack of hygiene, and lack of fulfilling your responsibilities. All these create a spiral effect on your relationships with family and friends, which can impact your career, goals, and every other area of your life... if you let them.

How can we shift those LVF? We can't jump up to the twentieth rung on a ladder when we are standing on the ground. However, we can step up one rung at a time. So going from being depressed to joy for some may be that elusive twentieth rung.

The recommendation is to think of something that you're grateful for, that makes you feel calmer, or puts a smile on your face. It can be as simple as thinking about your pet, a flower, etc. Gratitude is a higher vibration frequency (HVF) which comes from the heart.

Everyone can find one thing they are grateful for each day (the warmth of the sun, your bed you sleep in, etc.). The goal is to feel at least some comfort or peace at this stage. Start by practicing gratitude every day.

You can start simply, such as stating what you are grateful for out loud and/or write it down. Create a gratitude journal. Keep it in a place where you can easily reach for it during your daily routine so it truly becomes a regular practice.

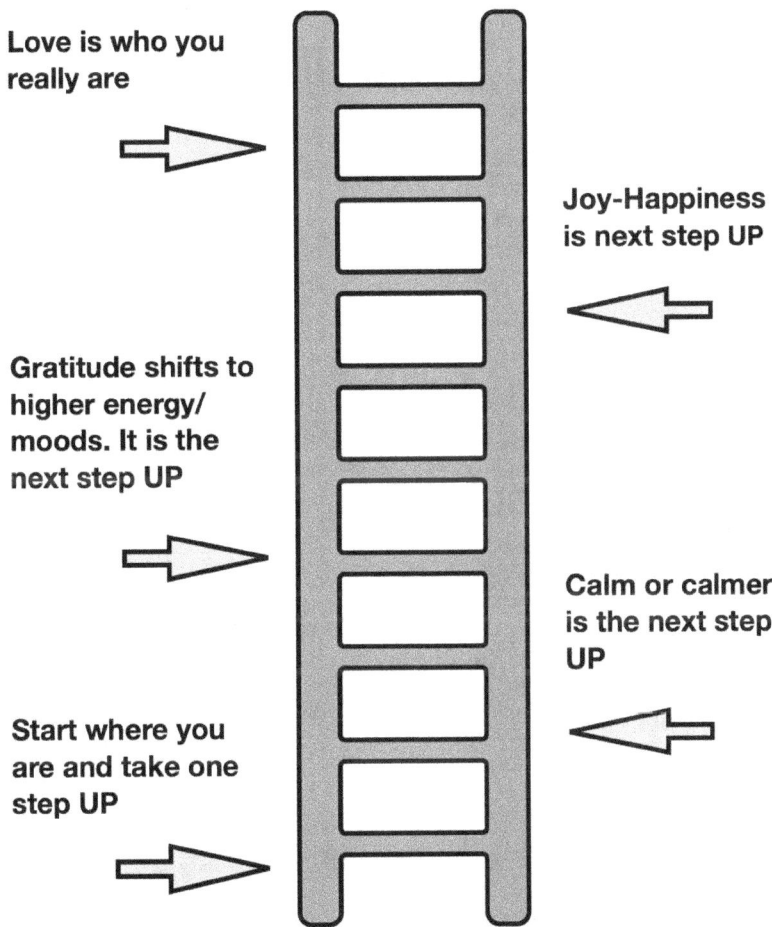

Love is who you really are

Joy-Happiness is next step UP

Gratitude shifts to higher energy/ moods. It is the next step UP

Calm or calmer is the next step UP

Start where you are and take one step UP

Chapter Five

Failure – Or Is It?

The word *failure* has such a bad rap. We will never be great at **everything** we try and learn in life. To fail is in fact to be human, and the only way we ever learn and grow.

It reminds me of Tigger in *Winnie-the-Pooh*, when he exclaimed, *"Tiggers are great at everything!"* Then he tried swimming and he realized he wasn't, so he simply stated from his rational mind, *"Tiggers are not great at swimming."* Tigger had the positive attitude to try it, it didn't work well for him so he moved on to the next thing he is great at. Humans often fail at something then attach all sorts of self-deprecating thoughts, such as, *"See, I knew I wouldn't be good enough!"* (Or smart enough, fast enough, strong enough, etc).

Let's look at athletes as an example of how failure can actually be a series of successes. Athletes will train for most of the year for their *"A Race"*, which is their most important race of the year. However, when they arrive at the race any number of factors could influence their performance: weather, sleep from the night before, hydration, food intake, nerves, etc. Whatever it is, sometimes the race just doesn't go their way. Olympic professional level and local level athletes have all experienced this at one time or another. Is this a failure? Well, many athletes could think so. The fact that the athlete was dedicated and met many smaller marks on their way to the "A Race" in my book is a success.

We are taught at a very young age about failure. It starts in our first twelve years of school when we don't make *the grade*. If one chooses to go to college the ongoing subtle stress levels of making *the grade* continues. Business owners experience losses and can easily deem them as failures. Marriages break up, children fall into trouble with the law, etc. There are so many examples in day-to-day life where one could deem themselves as a failure.

If one labels himself or herself a failure it creates an emotional, creative, mental and physical block. Like the *poor me* mindset, this can result in putting oneself into a slower, lower vibrational energy, which prolongs one's inability to pick themselves up again and move on.

How to be Friends with Failure

First off, externals (i.e. people, places, things, and situations) do not define you. Externals may create an initial emotion, which is normal, which leads to an initial thought (usually negative), which is also normal. However, you can acknowledge these thoughts as they arise, and then challenge them. After all, you are the boss of your thoughts, even if you didn't know that at first. It is your thoughts about the externals, not the externals themselves, nor the emotions that come up, that can cause you duress. Shift the thoughts to **facts**, literally just the facts.

You can choose to attach yourself to those unhappy feelings of failing or you can choose to view it more from a neutral space. Better yet you can thank them for being a catalyst to go in a new direction. A wonderful saying is, *"Nothing happens **to** you, it happens **for** you."* We often do not see it at the time it is happening, however as time goes on (sometimes years), we realize it was the best thing that could have happened for us. It is the journey where we gain all the knowledge, growth and wisdom. So fail and fail often.

In simpler terms, *learning* is making mistakes to understand what not to do or teaching you to choose something different next time. Mistakes and failing are both in the same wheelhouse as learning! You don't know what you don't know. So be wrong often because there is great power in that.

EXTERNALS

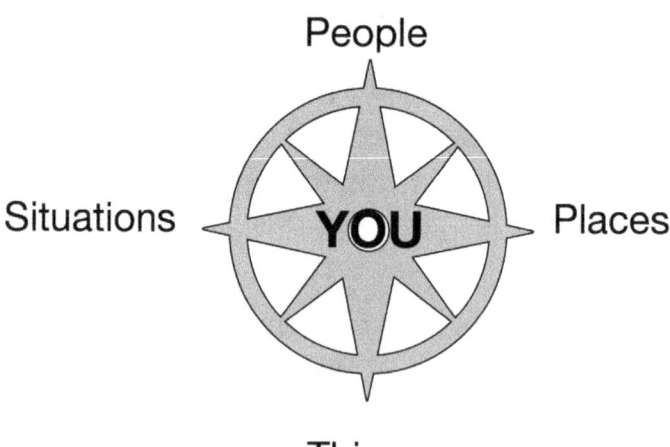

Externals do not control you, and
you do not control them

Chapter Six

Feelings

All feelings are neither good nor bad. Let's explore some of the more challenging ones and how to deal with them in a healthy way.

Anger

Yes, I know most people think anger is bad; it is not, it is what you do with the anger that can lead to issues. Anger actually is an emotion that can quickly be released, as long as you release it in a healthy way. When you do this you are giving it permission to be set free and flow through you. The opposite is holding onto it by retelling the story over and over, holding a grudge, not forgiving, wanting to get back at the other, etc. Any and all of those only truly hurt you, not the other person.

Holding anger causes the body to actively engage in survival mode, it deprives you of being present, being able to come up with solutions, or coming up with proactive steps. Worse, it wreaks havoc on the body and may show up in a variety of somatic ways (i.e. headaches, upset stomach, muscle tension, unable to fall asleep, clenched jaw, etc.). It lowers your immune system and could affect your relationships, your job, your self-esteem, and so on.

Anger is easier to react to and often covers up the *real* emotion under the anger. Anger is like the tip of the iceberg. Learning to be more aware of the truth of what you are feeling will help you immensely to grow as a person and to communicate better.

Tools for Anger:

A healthy release of anger is great: yell out loud when you're alone, scream into a pillow, jump up and down until you're exhausted, punch a pillow on your bed or your couch as fast as you can. The physical exertion can release anger within minutes. You then can identify the real emotions that originally created the anger.

Sadness

Sadness is a LVF and quickly needs to be acknowledged, comforted and released. Is it ok to be sad? Just like anger the answer is a resounding **yes**. There are various forms of sadness. With the case of grief, sadness can be an emotion of endearment. We would not feel sadness at the loss of someone if we did not love them. Tears from grief are what I call *love tears*. They are a reflection of your divine connection to the one you lost. Honor those tears. Don't try to hold onto it or stuff it down. Provide yourself some self-care and self-love by doing something for you that feels comforting.

You can also mourn losing a part of yourself when you let go of something that no longer serves you. If you have identified with a former part of yourself from the past which you have known for years, the shifting into a newness can cause the mourning of old you. When you have grown and moved on emotionally, spiritually, and/or physically, it is ok and a good thing.

Tools for sadness:

- Hold space for it, let it be what it is.

- It's ok to be uncomfortable, it's ok to feel off.

- Work through the feelings without attaching any kind of judgements or attempts to cover it up with unhealthy behaviors, or by pretending it doesn't exist.

- Honor that person and perhaps do something special in remembrance of them.

- Remember this phrase, *"The tree's gift is it holds onto nothing and bends with the storm."* (from the Little Book of Buddha). The quote means to allow sadness to come and go. As the storms blow through the trees, they do not fight it. Instead, they bend to the flow of the winds.

Anxiety

Anxiety is so prevalent in our society. It always was present, but since the Covid pandemic happened in 2020, anxiety has reached new heights from young children through seniors. In fact the pandemic severed the stigma of mental health and highlighted the important role mental health plays in our society. This is a good thing, but a lot of people still need help recognizing and managing their anxiety.

Anxiety is so misunderstood in the context of how one can be empowered to work with and through it. Often as soon as anxiety is felt it is equally matched with discomfort and resistance, which can include fear, anger, somatic issues, etc. One often finds themselves feeling powerless whether it is social anxiety, generalized anxiety, separation anxiety or the other forms of diagnostic anxiety. It can render one into a fight, flight or freeze mode, all due to the beliefs around anxiety.

Developing a tolerance to a certain level of anxiety is normal. For example, we can't control the weather so we adjust to it. Or, we get a paper cut and know that every time we wash our hands it will burn, but we wash our hands anyway because it keeps us healthy. We are excited about performing but the day of the performance we get some performance anxiety and have to work through it. This level of anxiety is good because it lets us know we are very much alive and human. When we challenge ourselves to work through anxiety it helps us to grow and instill confidence that we can and will do it again.

Tools for Anxiety:

Reframe anxiety in a new light: Instead of getting hung up on the feeling, focus on the neutral facts around the feeling.

- Fact: Anxiety is just an emotion.

- Fact: Hugging or sitting close to someone you love for thirty seconds or longer releases the hormone oxytocin in the body, which lowers our anxiety, relaxes our muscles and lowers our blood pressure.[3]

- Fact: Anxiety will pass

- Fact: Although anxiety arises it doesn't mean it has to stop us.

- Fact: If I choose to simply acknowledge anxiety out loud, it loses some of its power over me. I am then owning it, it doesn't own me.

- Fact: Anxiety comes up to help us work through something.

- Fact: There are many magic tools to implement any-time when we are feeling anxious. Pause to remember what they are.

- Fact: False smiles and real smiles are connected to our amygdala (the emotional part of our brain). A fake smile releases the same neurotransmitters (dopamine and serotonin), as does a real smile. So use it as a tool to shift anxiety.[4]

Another strategy is to start with counting backwards from five. This shifts the brain out of its emotional parts, known as the basal ganglia and the amygdala, and into the prefrontal cortex. The prefrontal cortex is our neutral zone. It works only with facts, figures, counting, clarity, organization, focus, solutions, etc. It is incapable of working at the same time as the emotional brain. So consciously shift to the prefrontal cortex quickly and often. It will improve your overall quality of life and well being, as you learn to become a master of your own emotions and thoughts.

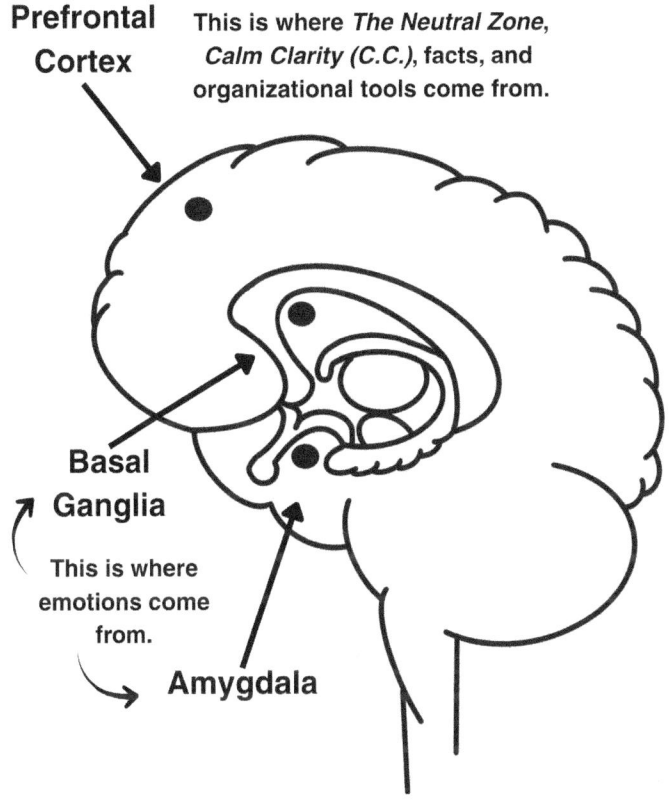

Prefrontal Cortex — This is where *The Neutral Zone*, *Calm Clarity (C.C.)*, facts, and organizational tools come from.

Basal Ganglia — This is where emotions come from.

Amygdala

Let's face it, there will be some events in life that will shake us up, knock us down and turn us around. Emotions can have a wide range of intensity, from daily small doses, to sudden shocking bursts, to a prolonged duration. These tools offer a way of finding your way back to yourself, while still feeling the emotions and allowing them to flow through you, without identifying **you** as the emotion.

Chapter Seven

Love or Fear

There are only two main emotions: fear or love. One can't exist at the same time as the other, which is a powerful thing. Love gives us many positive feelings such as happiness, compassion, and creativity, which all resonate from HVF and come from the heart. Your job is to move closer to any of those emotions as soon as you can. Embracing reality rather than resisting the externals will bring peace and a chance for you to shift into action and clarity. With radical acceptance, it creates space for creative options and solutions to the situation.

With fear we experience anger, loneliness, sadness, jealousy, overwhelm, anxiety, etc. Thoughts become reality. Check and challenge your thoughts about these emotions, watch your story you attach to them because it can feed the fire of fear and increase its intensity. Fear is predominantly made up stuff that doesn't even exist because it is in the future. Really think about how profound of a fact that is. Fear starts with sentences like, *"What if this?"* or *"What if that?"* etc. Until things are really coming to pass, they are only in your imagination.

How to move through emotions: Acknowledge them aloud. Say, *"I am feeling angry, agitated, etc."* When you state it aloud to yourself or to another you automatically have told the ego you are now taking over, which means you have empowered yourself. Try to quickly get to a calmer, clear state by using tools (See tools for anxiety, pages 19 and 20). Then take an action step, decide what you want to do, or how you want to move through the emotion. This can include letting it go, talking to someone, revisiting it at a later time when you have calmed down, taking a short walk, or even punching a pillow if need be.

Making a decision to act is empowering. Indecisions lead to ambivalence, a low level of anxiety, decreased motivation and lowered self-esteem. In some Eastern cultures, there is no such word as *try*. You either do or you don't. In my practice all my clients are aware they are immediately challenged when they say the following: *"I don't know," "I'll try,"* and *"Maybe."*

Self confidence is built on trusting yourself to make decisions. If you make a decision and it didn't work out the way you wanted, make another. We grow and learn from mistakes, and getting things wrong and learning from it is necessary. We touch a hot pan, we know not to do that again. We learn a new problem and get the answer wrong, wonderful because now we can learn what the right answer is.

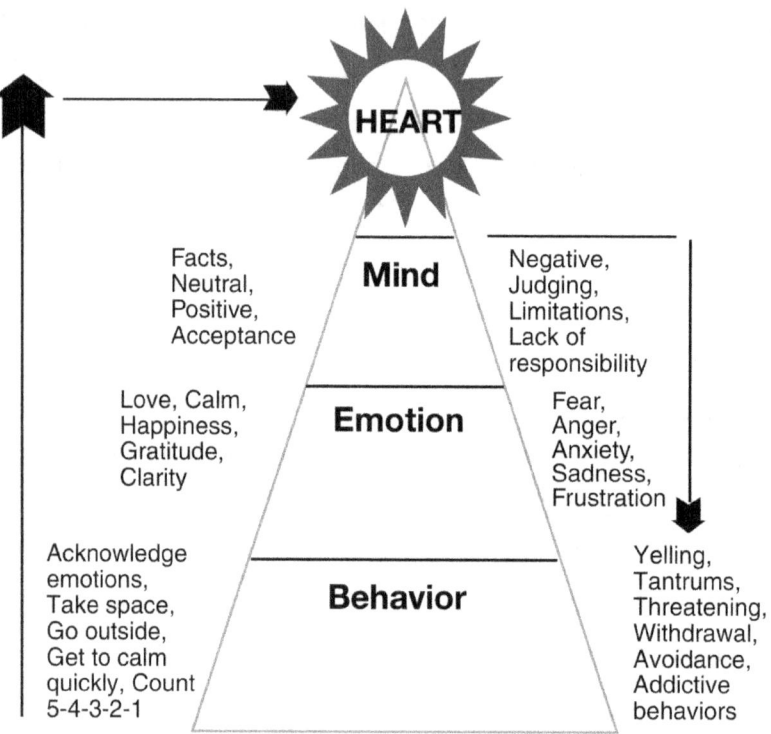

It is not the emotions that get us tripped up - it is the thoughts about the emotions that we keep retelling ourselves. We always have a choice on what we focus on. What we focus on will grow, as evidenced by the above.

Chapter Eight

The Neutral Zone

Humans make things so much harder than they need to be. There can be a different way to look at life by seeing it in a lighter way—through *The Neutral Zone*. Choose to let the small things go, see the humor and consciously smile more.

Start with neutral observation, by using the phrase, *"Isn't it interesting?"* For example, you might say, *"Isn't it interesting that my business partner is leaving?"* or *"Isn't it interesting that my boyfriend or girlfriend or partner decided to cheat on me?"*

Before we can implement *The Neutral Zone*, one usually has an initial reaction to an external. Reaction comes from emotions and the first and easiest emotion is anger. Anger is the tip of the iceberg. The true size of the iceberg is underneath the surface of the water. Anger masks our true feelings, such as hurt, fear, frustration, etc.

How long do we stay in anger? How long do we stay in the hurt or pain? How many times do we retell the story to others or post it on social media, or let it live rent free in our heads? How many nights of sleep do we lose? How are we consciously or unconsciously taking it out on others or ourselves? How is it affecting our day to day life and our relationships?

The more we choose to charge the energy and hold onto the energy of a negative emotion the more it wreaks havoc on our body, mind, spirit and all the other areas of our life. Many go into the *poor me* song again which, as we have explored, activates the lower energies.

So back to *The Neutral Zone*. When dealing with emotions, as quickly as possible go to facts after your initial processing.

- Neutral fact: Can you change what happened or what another is choosing to do? NO.

- Neutral Fact: Can you control anyone's thoughts, feelings, emotions or actions? NO.

- Neutral Fact: Does blaming yourself change anything? NO.

- Neutral Fact: Does attaching to poor me and staying disempowered serve you or others? NO.

Tools to move on to Radical Reframing:

- Radical Reframing: Something, or someone better is coming my way.

- Radical Reframing: Nothing happens **to** you, it happens **for** you.

- Radical Reframing: *"Thank you for helping me see this, even if I can't find the reason why this has happened. I know I will benefit from it and it is for my highest good and the good of all."*

At the end of the day, *The Neutral Zone* is about acceptance. The sooner we can let go of attachments, accept what is, and start releasing the emotionality, the sooner the shift to *The Neutral Zone*, which will create the higher vibrations of self-empowerment.

**Neutral Zone
a more balanced state**

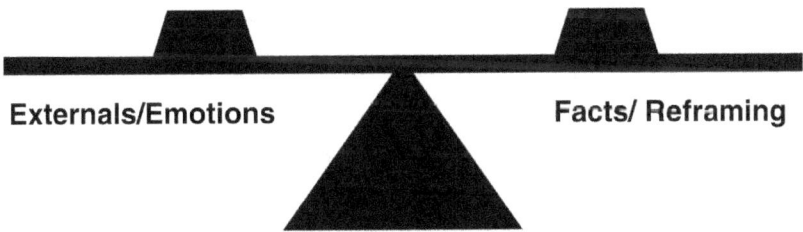

Externals/Emotions   Facts/ Reframing

Chapter Nine

Empowerment

This is one of my favorite quotes:

"Ego says when everything falls into place, I'll have peace. Spirit says when I have peace everything falls into place. "
~Marianne Williamson

Externals (people, places, things, situations and events), are not our source of empowerment or peace - quite the opposite. If you allow the externals to define you, your moods, or your value, then you have essentially made yourself a victim. This holds true for every environment.

Empowerment is not being *in control* of everything and everyone. Empowerment is knowing you have zero control over all the externals. Empowerment is being able to be open to allow all the externals to be as they are when they arise. There is their stuff, your stuff and God's stuff (or the universe's stuff, whatever you want to insert there). Focus only on **your** stuff.

The courage, strength and work is to understand that it is not for you to judge the externals or become attached to them. It is for you to catch how much energy you are investing in them and for how long. Then begin the process of releasing and letting go of what you can not control.

Here's an example. On your way to work a speeding driver tailgates you, then passes you and cuts in front of you. Most people experience a situation to some degree as the following: there is the initial reaction of being alert, an increase in hyper-vigilance to stay safe, and then a hit of the emotion. Anger usually is what follows the incident. How long and to what level of anger does one take it? The choice is yours.

Empowerment is going through all those steps and then letting it go as quickly as it happened. Empowerment can then be further enhanced with reframing of different words (yes, those choice words we yell aloud when we are alone). Instead try, *"Isn't that interesting that happened? Thank you for keeping me safe."* There is a full spectrum of possibilities making it so we don't know why that person was driving like that. We often will jump quickly to negative judgment to justify what happened.

Try reframing those thoughts. Maybe this person found out his daughter just was brought to the hospital, or his father fell and called him for help. It is actually irrelevant as to why it happened - the **fact** is it did, and now, how can you move through it quickly?

My quote I coined and say often with my clients is, *"Empowerment comes from Calm Clarity (C.C.)."*

Being in *Calm Clarity* is to be in the place of answers, being able to take action, being non-emotional and being able to state, share, and advocate for yourself without attachment to what others may say, feel, or do. C.C. is where your intuition, your inner source, your guidance, and your place of connectedness lies and is found only in the heart. When you come from that place you and everyone or everything else benefits. Seek to shift out of the emotional brain and into the prefrontal cortex where you can then easily slide into C.C.

Someone could be angry with you, yelling at you and being down right unreasonably reactive. Empowerment is not feeding into their fire. If you feed the fire that person will inevitably get more heightened, as will you, which always becomes a lose-lose communication. There is no resolution in that state. A simple validation of the others feelings can take them down a notch. Try saying something like, *"I understand and hear that you are mad about this or at me. I need some space to think about it. "*

Empowerment is never having to justify yourself, especially repeatedly. If you are coming from your truth and speaking with C.C. then that **is** the power, the grace, the gift you've given yourself and even the other person, despite them not being able to realize it.

Empowerment is relinquishing the *need* to be right. Can you agree to disagree? The *need* is the ego working hard to give you a false sense of security.

I love this saying, *"Would you rather be right or would you rather have peace?"* It is really okay to agree to disagree. Empowerment is focusing on the solutions and not the problem. The longer one focuses on the problem the bigger it gets and the further away from C.C. that one becomes. Being solution focused is an action based step. Actions empower and motivate us to move forward. What you put your attention on grows.

Empowerment is always about choice. Own the choice you've made no matter what it is, and if you don't like the results simply make another choice.

Take 100% responsibility for you, no matter what.

Allow me to expand on this. Empowerment is owning your actions, thoughts, words, behaviors, feelings and choices. It matters not if it was appropriate, kind, mean, reactive, etc. You are living with you and no one can **make** you do, say, feel or act without **your** permission.

It is easy to fall into a blaming mindset, such as thinking, *"They used me"* or *"They manipulated me."*

If that is your triggered reaction then it is about learning to rewire our brains with a different mindset. It is about learning to be more connected to your true source of empowerment. Truly wanting to change is the first step. Then working to find support if needed to change is the next.

Electronics and Their Role

People are so busy being busy that they rarely pause to just be still, let alone be with themselves without distractions. We live in a world where everything and everyone is literally at your fingertips through electronics. There are two sides to our technology, one very different from the other.

Social media has opened up a whole new world, one where parasocial relationships feel real, and real relationships can slip away. The trick is having the awareness of which one you are involved in, and is predominantly in your life!

Social media can also impact your sense of self worth. If you are focusing on how many likes, comments, reviews, etc, you are getting, you may feel disappointment, rejected or even more isolation.

Mindless scrolling can also create a diversion away from the self. When one has the fear of missing out (FOMO), it is an indicator of an external need to fill an internal void. If you have to sleep with the cell phone in your room, if you have to look at it first thing upon waking, if you are checking it while you are in the company of friends and family, if everything you do has to be posted, you are disconnecting with the reality in front of you in exchange for the electronic one in your hand. These are all indicators of FOMO. Overuse of electronics does not help improve focus, in fact, it is the opposite. It causes many children, teenagers and even adults to struggle being present. It decreases communication and socialization skills in person, whether in school, at home or in public settings. Teenage suicide has even been linked to excessive use of electronics and electronics addictions. [5]

The other side of electronics is much more positive. They can be a great source of information. They can connect people to each other who would not be able to otherwise connect with. They can provide ways for like-minded groups to share their interests, sports, hobbies, academic achievements and research. They can help enhance and expand business. You can learn about the world, and find many choices for social, emotional, physical, and educational development. All of that is good, however a healthy balance is required when using electronics.

Tools for Electronics:

Use a timer to set a goal of social and business media responses. For example, determine an allotted timeframe for each task, such as ten to fifteen minutes for clearing emails, or thirty minutes for research. Make sure you take a break every forty-five to sixty minutes before the brain goes into what I call a *fogged over* mode. That means you have been affected by the electromagnetic waves emanating from all screens and are almost in a tranced mode. This decreases learning, memory retention, and overall effectiveness. It can also cause stress, anger, frustration and tiredness. When you are in those states you have now activated your sympathetic nervous responses of arousal. Continuing to stay on screens at that point will only increase those unhealthy somatic responses.

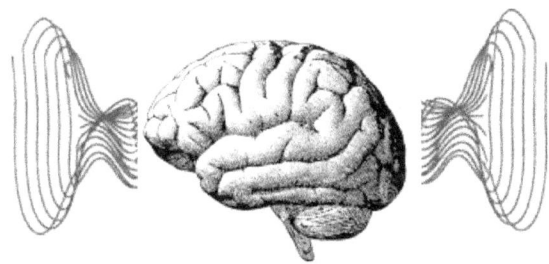

Electromagnetic frequencies still active in the brain after disconnecting

Just because we disconnect from electronics does not mean our brain stops firing from the effects of the exposure to the electromagnetic waves. The neural activity in the brain continues so it needs time to slip into the parasympathetic nervous system (our calming part of our nervous system). So when the timer on your phone goes off—**stop**. You will feel successful in being able to discipline yourself while still accomplishing a goal and having more energy and clarity, therefore being more productive.

Take a break, get away, splash water on your face, get a snack, and do something else before returning. This will support your overall well being and productivity.

Your Source

Empowerment means being aware of and connected to your source.

Source is your heart chakra, or your internal source of power and love. It is endless, limitless and available to you every moment. It is where you find *Calm Clarity* (C.C.), your true creative source, empathy, kindness, gratitude and where you are always enough. Know you are always more than enough. The grace and beauty of this is that even when we stray as humans we can find our way back. Back to ourselves!

Our place of empowerment has no judgment of self or others, is unattached to outcomes, and is about **being more** instead of **doing more**. It is finding stillness to allow miracles to show up, for the next creative idea, the solution, or the next adventure you must go on. This is your truth and learning to live, speak, and be it, is worth aspiring for. This is when true meaningful, real physical relationships and connections happen. When you are in alignment with your source, people, places, situations, and things start to show up to support your truth, your path, and your goals.

There is no such thing as coincidences. Most people have to get out of their own way. I challenge you to not be afraid of your light. Practice some of what was learned in this book on a daily basis. Start with one simple step. Dreams are only entertainment unless you act on them. You will succeed if you are both disciplined and determined. Why? Because even if you don't know it, you are limitless. Everything you need to succeed has always been in you. Just like Dorothy in the original Wizard of Oz movie, she had the magic shoes on her feet the entire journey. She always had the power. And so do you.

Chapter Ten

A Different Way

It is time for me to share my magical tools that you can add to your daily life to ensure that you are living a more empowered life.

However, it is crucial for you first to ask, *"How important is it for me to have more peace and feel more empowered in my life?"* Changes and growth won't happen unless you are willing to create space for it. Mindfulness is all about the practice of being present. It takes conscious effort for anything to become unconscious.

An example that most people can relate to is learning how to drive a car. Your brain is working hard to remember everything. At first you drive slow and look more than two times to turn. You are in the process of building new neural networks in your brain through repetition. But eventually it all becomes second nature and you drive the car almost effortlessly.

It may take up to thirty days to develop a new habit, it is not an overnight process. It is the same with driving. The more you practice driving the more confident you become in trusting yourself. You drive with more speed and your brain isn't over-thinking every step. Eventually the act of driving slips into the subconscious. That is until we have a bad winter storm or heavy rains and you find yourself once again fully alert at the task of driving with the new conditions from the road. But now you have the skills, and even though it takes effort, you can meet the challenge successfully.

This is exactly why we need to develop a solid base of self-care, self-love, and mindfulness daily practice. That way, when life takes a twist or turn, you can draw upon that base to get through things in a more stable, peaceful way.

Chapter Eleven

Morning Routine

When we first awaken, our brains are in an alpha state which is linked with being very relaxed, and with passive attention. Passive attention is when we receive information without actively trying to focus. For example, when we hear the sounds of nature, the information is received in our brain and processed passively. It is the perfect time for learning new spiritual, enlightened information, for going within, for creative time, and a time of observation of nature and the world around us. How you chose to start your day, will set the tone for the day, so be mindful of your choices.

It is important to understand that prior to expending your energy to others, first thing in the a.m., spend time with **you**. Prior to doing chores or tasks, fill your cup up first. No, that absolutely does **not** mean any form of social media, emails, TV, or any form of electronics. Avoid those during this time. Provide yourself a time in the a.m. to ground yourself in body, mind and spirit. This can be as short as ten minutes or as long as needed to give yourself the gift of uninterrupted time. You and everyone around you will benefit, and your day is more likely to go smoother. You may even find yourself more efficient and productive. There is nothing that can't be done better than by doing it in a calm state or C.C., and that is what a base of self-care and self-love will provide.

Magic Tools (a.m.)

- Your cup of coffee or tea sitting quietly indoors or outdoors and enjoying the stillness

- Yoga or stretching

- Meditating

- Consciously take longer, slower deep breaths

- Sit outside in nature, which provides natural grounding and soothing for the soul

- Tune into your surroundings. Look, really look, around outside your own window or door and **see** the changes in mother earth, listen to the noises, feel the temperatures, smell the scents. Use your five senses to be present

- Embrace gratitude - verbally state out loud what you are grateful for in your own surroundings and life and make a practice of doing this daily

- Smiling and/or laughing more - look for a simple thing that can put a smile on your face when you think of it

- Listening to morning affirmations, which will set the tone for the day

- Take a short walk to clear off the sleep fog

- Any form of exercise followed by some still, quiet time

- Sit by the water if that is possible

- Reading a self-help, spiritual or inspiration book for ten minutes

- Coloring, writing, dancing, drawing, painting, playing music, any creative and or artistic endeavor

- Any craft/hobby projects such as knitting, wood working, and gardening

Chapter Twelve

Evening Routine

It is equally important to develop an evening routine as it is a morning mindfulness routine. Our body, mind and spirit needs to release, relax and reconnect after a day of continual stimulation and stressors. Many people go on autopilot to get tasks done (making dinner, cleaning up, getting the kids ready for bed, doing laundry, etc.). Are those things part of daily life? But of course! What I am suggesting is **how** you go about all the above.

Can you introduce music, singing, or creative opportunities to your daily tasks to make them fun? Have you ever noticed the more you rush the more it seems you are running out of time? I have found that the more present and relaxed I am at doing all things, the easier they flow, the quicker they seem to get done, and the more time I have. The best part is I am expending less energy because I am calmer. The other benefit is the more fully present you are, the more accomplished you feel for getting the tasks done with increased ease. Imagine feeling that way with every task.

Electronics Again...

The evening comes and people are back on their electronics right up until the time they go to bed. All electronics emanate electromagnetic frequencies which keep the brain alert and fired up. It is the reason why children and adults can be addicted to them so easily, it is like a drug that, once activated, wants more.

The brain activity does **not** shut off when you shut off the electronics. The brain activity continues to fire which is why many have a hard time falling asleep. It is so crucial to disconnect at least 45 minutes before going to bed. This will slow down the neural firing in our brain, which will allow the body to slip into the parasympathetic nervous system, which is our calming system. Electronic usage affects our bodies as well as our emotional states of well being. Disconnecting before bed is giving ourselves permission to reconnect to ourselves and our natural internal states of well being. This sets ourselves up for a good night's sleep and a better morning.

Watching violent or scary games, TV shows, YouTube videos, TikTok videos, etc., has significant effects on our mind, body responses, and thoughts. I see too many clients, both children and adults who have difficulty falling asleep, are afraid of going to sleep, have fear of the dark, have bad dreams, nightmares, and restless night's sleep. The images and sounds create neural imprints. Since negative images result in negative responses, the opposite will be true when you immerse yourself with soothing happy sounds or images.

Magic Tools (p.m.)

- Disconnect with all electronics forty-five minutes or more prior to going to bed

- Listen to music without words

- Listen to evening affirmations

- Meditate

- Read, but not on a screen

- Make a puzzle

- Do any craft projects

- Color, draw or create

- Play a board or card game with someone

- Sit outside

- Go for an early evening walk or hike

- Garden a bit

- Reflect on your day and find three things to be thankful for - they can be simple things which are often the best (i.e. seeing a butterfly, having a laugh at something, a nice conversation, etc.)

- Write in a journal

- Have a cup of decaffeinated or herbal tea

- Have an actual conversation face to face with some-one (what was good about the day, plan a future fun event, etc.)

Chapter Thirteen

Final Empowering Thoughts

This book was intentionally made to be small so it can travel with you wherever you go. It can serve as a helpful reminder of how to become empowered and continually apply these tools into your daily life. However, it requires your own personal discipline to create a new mindful based life, and this starts first with awareness.

Ask yourself, *"How am I expending my energy?"* If you find yourself expending it being stressed, tired, rushing, anxious, doing more than being, remind yourself that it is a choice. Believe it or not, all our things we need to do or want to do can be accomplished in a calmer state of being and with much more success. If you can spend ten minutes stressed out, can you spend ten minutes being calm? Where do you want to invest your energy?

Mindfulness is a continual practice which reaps incredible results, often in a short amount of time. Every new thing, new habit, and new neural networks created in the brain takes conscious effort. All things are practiced in a repeated consistent manner, before they slip into our subconscious where it becomes a state of grace and ease. Think of it as building your own personal base of internal support. Just as a building is only as solid as its foundation, or a tree its roots, your own daily base will help you stand strong. Continually honor that base by setting time for it.

You will be surprised how this will change your life in ways that have far greater rewards than you can possibly imagine. You will find yourself seeking the time alone and it becomes in time a non-negotiable part of your life. The rewards show up in externals, when people, places, things, or situations come and go and you are able to be present for them, accept things more easily, set healthy boundaries for yourself, advocate for yourself, and move through it all much quicker.

Begin small which will provide a level of adjustment and manageability. Start with developing an a.m. routine of just ten minutes for **you time**. Do that consistently before adding on. After a few weeks or up to a month, add the additional ten minute routine to your evening and stick with that consistently. Then, build onto those bases. You may find your own creative use for **you time**.

All of my clients have reported feeling increased peace in their day to day packed lives. They have also reported that they feel a shift when they stop their daily base (falling back in anxiety, anger, etc.), resulting in being less calm, clear, organized and grounded.

I can guarantee you if you develop new habits in the a.m. and the p.m., you will find in time an increased more consistent state of peace settle within your soul. I will also share that once these practices are in place and you are feeling an overall increased well-being, you will *want* to do them. Once you feel a new more balanced way of being in the world you rarely want to go back to the old way. But it will take discipline!

I know you can do this, peace is an inside job and we must be the peace we seek and feel to have it returned back to us. What you seek is seeking you. You have to allow the quiet space to open your heart to let it in and know you are worthy of it.

Most live from their heads (or *ego*), which thrives on keeping you in the fight, flight or freeze mode. The ego is self-deprecating, judgmental and loves to keep us limited and stuck in life, void of trust, and all the possibilities that exist for us. It doesn't have to be that way!

Through these daily practices you are internally connecting to your heart. When done on a consistent basis, you develop: increased capacity to make healthy choices, healthy boundary setting, trusting yourself and your intuition, increased self-esteem, creativity, an ability to find solutions and deal with challenges, and improved overall sense of well-being.

Externally, your relationships, work, playtime, productivity, athletic endeavors, and appreciation of life and nature will all improve. Energy attracts like energy, so watch in appreciation and awe as you travel down this new path of empowerment. You will be supported in wonderful ways, ways you could not have possibly imagined.

In closing, I would like to leave you with empowering mantras that I use in my personal life and with my clients. May they also bring you peace and empowerment!

"Live fully now, by committing to be more present in your life every day."

"Do something new, limitations are self-imposed."

"Everything you need is and has always been inside you...set it free."

"Step into your new empowered life and develop your innate natural superpower, Calm Clarity (C.C.)"

" Enjoy the process."

Much light, love, and peace on your journey.

~Lisa

Afterword

As you close this book, take a moment to acknowledge something powerful: you've just given yourself the gift of awareness, tools, and support for living a more empowered life. Whether you've read this cover to cover or flipped to the sections you needed most, the real transformation begins now—with your daily practice.

You now have a toolbox filled with simple, accessible strategies for calming your nervous system, reframing negative thoughts, and reconnecting to your sense of self. You've learned how to shift from reaction to reflection, from overwhelm to intentionality. Best of all, you've done it in your own way, at your own pace.

Here are just a few of the key things to remember as you move forward:

- Reclaim your calm in moments of stress

- Reframe your thinking when negativity creeps in

- Build emotional resilience

- Strengthen your relationship with yourself

- Respond to life with more intention and grace

Keep this book nearby to return to the tools when life gets loud. Empowerment is not a destination. It's a practice, a mindset, and a way of being. And now, it's yours. Whether you use one technique or all of them, trust that change happens through repetition, self compassion, and showing up—even on messy days.

Thank you for taking this journey. You are the creator of your own reality.

Key Takeaways to Remember:

- You are allowed to feel your emotions without being defined by them.

- Empowerment begins with awareness – and grows with practice.

- There's no "right" timeline for healing or growth.

- You already have what you need within you – you're just remembering how to access it.

- Your daily choices shape your future self.

Reflection Questions:

Take a few quiet moments to consider the following:

1. Which tools or techniques from this book resonated most with me?

2. How do I currently respond to stress and my emotions? What would I like to do differently?

3. What does empowerment mean to me—personally and practically?

4. In what areas of my life do I feel the most confident? Where do I want to grow?

5. What's one thing I can start doing daily to feel more grounded, intentional, or empowered?

Journaling Prompt:

"The most important lesson I'm taking with me from this book is..."

Let yourself write freely, without judgment. Your truth is your greatest guide.

Final words:

Empowerment isn't about having all the answers—it's about being willing to pause, reflect, and choose again. Keep this book close. Come back to it as often as you need. You are not behind. You are becoming.

And that is something worth celebrating.

About the Author

Lisa is a Licensed Professional Counselor and a Registered Art Therapist, with a successful private practice in Vernon, CT. Lisa is a dynamic speaker with topics ranging from self-empowerment, to parenting and coaching skills. She is an author, artist and an athlete. Lisa was the designer and facilitator of the Sandy Hook Memorial Fountain, installed in Portland, CT. This was a project which took three years to be completed. In her spare time, Lisa is a triathlete and enjoys taking on new athletic challenges each year. She enjoys all outdoors activities and traveling. She enjoys creating art and regularly partakes in art exhibits in her local community.

Connect With Lisa

Websites:
www.TouchedByArt.net
www.TouchedByArtTherapy.com
Email:
touchedbyart@yahoo.com
Social Media:
Instagram: @LBconnect3

Resources

Books:

Behrend, Genevieve. *Your Invisible Power*.

Dispenza, Joe. *Becoming Supernatural: How Common People Are Doing the Uncommon*.

Dyer, Wayne W. *Change Your Thoughts—Change Your Life*.

Dyer, Wayne W. *Manifest Your Destiny: The Nine Spiritual Principles for Getting Everything You Want*.

Hay, Louise L. *You Can Heal Your Life*.

Ruiz, Don Miguel. *The Four Agreements: A Practical Guide to Personal Freedom*.

Singer, Michael A. *The Untethered Soul: The Journey Beyond Yourself*.

YouTube Videos:

Hicks, Abraham *Source is Always Focused on Your Success! – Pure Guidance*
https://youtu.be/1-MTNvDZQ9w

Morrissey, Mary *The Hidden Code for Transforming Dreams Into Reality – TEDxWilmingtonWomen*
https://www.youtube.com/watch?v=UPoTsudFF4Y

Winfrey, Oprah *Best Ever Motivational Speeches Compilation/Most Inspirational Video Ever:*
https://youtu.be/fxm3TYqD-Kw

Endnotes

Emotional Frequencies
1. The Whole Universe is Vibrating:
   https://www.youtube.com/watch?v=GLq3ffMprrw

2. The Power of Vibrational Frequency and Your
   Emotional Guidance System:
   https://bit.ly/40Dp0mw

Feelings
1. How do Hugs Make You Feel?:
   https://bit.ly/40Dp0mw

2. Smiling Can Trick Your Mind into Being More Positive:
   https://bit.ly/4fGgLdF

Empowerment
1. Smartphones, Social Media Use and Youth Mental
   Health:
   https://www.ncbi.nlm.nih.gov/pmc/articles/PMC701
   2622/)

www.ingramcontent.com/pod-product-compliance
Lightning Source LLC
Chambersburg PA
CBHW060353130626
46553CB00003B/1212